Table of Contents

Chapter 1 – Introduction to Accounting

Accounting Terms and Concepts

Before beginning the accounting material, it is important to understand the language, so a few basic terms and definitions will be covered. Definitions for any bolded terms can be found in the Glossary, located at back of the book.

In accounting, there are five main accounts. The first account is an **asset**. An asset is an item, tangible or intangible, that has economic value. Economic value can either mean that the asset itself is worth something, or that it has the ability to produce something of value. For example, a house has intrinsic value, but it can also produce value by means of rent. Within the asset account, there are several different subaccounts. **Current assets** are a class of asset that is easy to liquidate. For example, merchandise inventory is easy to liquidate by selling a unit or units. Accounts receivable (an account used to record monies owed to you) is easy to liquidate by collecting the amount owed or selling the debt. **Capital assets** (sometimes referred to as **long term assets** or **property, plant and equipment**) on the other hand are assets that are difficult to liquidate. For example, selling a house or a car is not as straight forward as selling merchandise inventory. Other characteristics of capital assets include having a deed or a title, and being depreciable. **Investments** are financial assets that bear a risk in exchange for making a reward. For example, when purchasing stocks on the stock market, there is a risk that they will go down in value but the rewards are that they go up in value and possibly pay dividend. Lastly, **intangible assets** are assets that cannot be physically touched. For example a company's logo is an intangible asset.

The next account is a **liability**. A liability is a future obligation resulting from a current transaction. A **current liability** is a liability that is due in the near future, typically within one year. For example, purchasing office supplies on account (current transaction) is creating a debt that will have to be settled (future obligation). Liabilities that are not due as soon, typically more than one year, are called **long-term liabilities**. A 20 year mortgage, for example, would be a long-term liability.

After liabilities comes **equity**. Equity is the amount of claim an owner has or partners have on the assets of a business. There are three types of equities. The first is **owner's equity**. Owner's equity is the account used for a **sole proprietorship**, which is an unincorporated business that only has one owner. The second one is **partners' equity**. Partners' equity is the account used for a **partnership**, which is an unincorporated business that has two or more owners. The third one is **shareholder's equity**. Shareholder's equity is the account used for a **corporation**, which is an incorporated business that has one or more owners.

Assets, liabilities and equity are the three accounts that appear on the balance sheet. The sum of the total liabilities and total equity is equal to the total assets. This is denoted as:

$$A = L + E$$

The fourth account is **revenue**, which is the gross amount of money earned by a business. Some of these revenues can include sales revenue, interest revenue and rental revenue.

The fifth and final main account is **expenses**, which are the total costs incurred by a business in order to earn revenue. For example, renting a factory to produce goods is a necessary expense to earn revenue.

Revenue and expenses are the two accounts that appear on the income statement. The total revenue, minus the total expenses is the **net income**. If the expenses exceed the revenues in a given period, the company will report a **net loss**. This is denoted as:

$$NI = R - E$$

There are two main types of accounting: **cash basis accounting** and **accrual basis accounting**. Cash basis accounting records revenues when cash is *received* and expenses when cash is *paid*. Accrual basis accounting records revenues when they are *earned* and expenses when they are *incurred*. To record the transactions of a business, **journal entries** are used. A journal entry is the basic record of a business' transaction. In order to prepare a journal entry, at least one **account** must be debited and at least one account must be credited. For each journal entry, the total debits and the total credits must be equal. That is, they must balance. This is called **double-entry accounting**. An account is a record where each of the transactions affecting that account will be recorded. Cash is an account, so each time the amount of cash that a business has changes, the cash account will be recorded to reflect each change. Each account has a **normal balance** which helps predict whether an account will be debited or credited.

Outside of accounting, **debits and credits** mean decreasing and increasing, respectively. For example, a withdrawal of $500 from a chequing account would show a debit of $500 on the statement. Likewise, a deposit of $500 into a chequing account would show a credit of $500. For the purposes of accounting, debit and credit can mean increasing or decreasing, depending on the account being affected. There are specific rules for each account which dictate whether a transaction is a debit record or a credit record. The following chart outlines these rules:

	Asset	Liability	Equity	Revenue	Expense
Increasing	Debit	Credit	Credit	Credit	Debit
Decreasing	Credit	Debit	Debit	Debit	Credit

To prepare a journal entry, look at the above chart. The intersection of the account being affected and whether it is increasing or decreasing will determine if it is a debit or credit. For example, when an asset account is increasing, the asset account is being debited. When an expense account is decreasing, the expense account is being credited. If a utilities bill was being paid, an asset account (cash) would be decreasing and an expense account (utilities expense) would be increasing. Therefore "Utilities Expense" would be debited and "Cash" would be credited, both in the amount of the bill being paid.

The "increasing" row is the row of normal balances. When it comes to normal balances, there is one exception known as **contra accounts**. Contra accounts have the opposite normal balances. For example, the normal balance of an asset is a debit. Therefore the balance of a contra asset is a credit.

Generally Accepted Accounting Principles

In accounting, there are certain principles that are followed to ensure that reporting is useful to internal and external users. These are called the **generally accepted accounting principles** (GAAP). The following chart outlines these principles:

Principle	Description
Business Entity Principle	The transactions that a business records, must not represent the personal transactions of the owner(s). For example, an owner cannot list the amount they spend on clothes as an expense on the business' income statement.
Consistency Principle	The same accounting methods must be used period after period. A company that uses one method to calculate the cost of inventory in January must use the same method in February. This allows readers to make comparisons throughout several different periods.
Cost Principle	Financial statement information to be based on the cost of a specific transaction. For example, if a car is purchased for $10, 000 but has a market value of $15, 000, the cost principle requires that $10, 000 be recorded.
Full Disclosure Principle	Financial statements must include all relevant information. If a business experienced a loss in one of its departments, the full disclosure principle prevents the owner from leaving that loss off the books
Matching Principle	Expenses must be reported in the same period as the revenues that were earned
Materiality Principle	Amounts may be left out of the financial statements if they will not be of interest to the reader. For example, if a business spent $1 on a stamp.
Revenue Recognition Principle	Revenue must be recorded at the time it is earned (when the good is delivered or the service is rendered), not when the payment is received.
Timeliness Principle	The business' transactions must be reported on a consistent basis. For example, quarterly, monthly or annually.

Understanding the Accounting Cycle and Analyzing Transactions

The accounting cycle is the full process completed bookkeepers, and the full cycle is completed once per period. If a company does its reporting monthly, there will be 12 accounting cycles per **fiscal year**. If the company does its reporting annually, there will be 1 accounting cycle per fiscal year. If a company does its reporting quarterly, there will be 4 accounting cycles per fiscal year. Not only can a company choose how many accounting cycles are done per fiscal year, but they can also choose when their own fiscal year end. For example, if a company choses to report quarterly and sets a year end of April 30, the quarters would run May 1 to July 31, August 1 to October 31, November 1 to January 31 and February 1 to April 30. While many businesses use the calendar year end as their fiscal year end, it is not ideal for some businesses. For example a seasonal business that has the most activity in the winter (i.e. a ski lodge), would have the calendar year end fall right in the middle of their busy season. A business like that would likely make their fiscal year-end around May 31.

The nine steps of the accounting cycle are shown below, along with which chapter will cover each step:

1. Analyze transactions (Chapter 1)
2. Journalize transactions (Chapter 2)
3. Post transactions (Chapter 2)
4. Unadjusted trial balance (Chapter 3)
5. Adjusting entries (Chapter 3)
6. Adjusted trial balance (Chapter 3)
7. Financial statements (Chapter 4)
8. Closing entries (Chapter 5)
9. Post-close trial balance (Chapter 5)

Steps 1 through 3 are all about the individual transactions. Making sure they are correct and then correctly recording them. Steps 4 to 6 involve totalling the transactions based on account, making any adjustments to the individual transactions and then updating the list. Step 7 is converting the information to financial statements, which are a critical form of communication between the business and its **stakeholders**. Steps 8 and 9 are closing temporary accounts at the year end so a new period can begin.

The first step, analyzing transactions, is exactly what it sounds like. The transactions that are being analyzed are found on the **source documents**. These include receipts, invoices, cash register tapes and employee punch cards. This is to make sure that everything is in good order, and that nothing has been tampered with or accidentally entered incorrectly. Once all of the source documents are in good order, the transactions are ready to be journalized.

Chapter 2 – Recording Transactions

Journalizing Transactions

Once the source documents are in good order, they are converted into journal entries by posting them to the **general journal**. Below is the layout of what a general journal looks like:

General Journal					
Date	Description		PR	Debit	Credit
(a)	(b)		(g)	(c)	
	(e)		(h)		(d)
	(f)				

(a) The month and date of the transaction. It is typically in "15 Dec." or "Dec. 15" format.

(b) The account being debited

(c) The amount that is being debited.

(d) The amount that is being credited.

(e) The account that is being credited.

(f) A description of the transaction that typically begins with *"To record ..."*

(g) The account number for the account being debited.

(h) The account number for the account being credited.

Each account has an account number (in the PR (post-reference) column) so that it may be easily found on the ledger. When a business starts up, a **chart of accounts** is created. This functions like a table of contents for the accounting department. The chart of accounts lists all accounts (grouped into assets, liabilities, equity, revenues and expenses) and an account number is assigned to each. If a business created a new account along the way, it is simply added to the chart of accounts. When coming up with account numbers, it is a good idea to leave a series of numbers between each account number. For example, if assets are the 100's (i.e. 101 is cash, 102 is accounts receivable, 103 is inventory, etc.) then liabilities in the 200's (i.e. accounts payable is 201, notes payable is 202, unearned revenue is 203, etc.). That way if a new asset account is created, such as office supplies, it can be assigned number 104 and it will be listed in the 100's with the other assets. Note that for the purposes of this book, assets will be the 100's, liabilities will be the 200's, equity will be the 300's, revenues will be the 400's and expenses will be the 500's. The following is an example of a chart of accounts:

(Company Name) Chart of Accounts		
Name of Account	Type of Account	Account Number
Cash	Current Asset	101
Office Supplies	Current Asset	102
Merchandise Inventory	Current Asset	103
Accounts Payable	Current Liability	201
Capital, J. Doe	Equity	301
Rental Revenue	Revenue	401
Telephone Expense	Expense	501

When doing a journal entry, look at the transaction and think about the following:

1. What accounts are being affected?

2. Are the accounts increasing or decreasing?

3. What are the normal balances of the accounts?

4. Based on #2 and #3, will this account be debited or credited?

Consider a company that purchased office supplies in the amount of $500 on June 21. The supplies were paid for in cash.

1. The accounts being affected are Cash (101) and Office Supplies (107).

2. The Office Supplies account is increasing (since they were purchased) and the Cash account is decreasing (since the purchase involves an outlay of cash).

3. Since both accounts are assets, the normal balance for both accounts is a debit.

4. Since the normal balance is a debit, the increasing asset (Office Supplies) will be debited while the decreasing asset (Cash) will be credited.

Based on the above information, the journal entry would appear as follows:

General Journal					
Date	Description	PR	Debit	Credit	
June 21	Office supplies	107	500		
	Cash	101		500	
	To record the cash purchase of office supplies				

Consider the same example as before, but instead of paying cash, the supplies were paid for on account which will be paid off at a later date. The company from whom the supplies were purchased is Barrie Business Supplies.

1. The accounts being affected are **Accounts Payable** (201) and Office Supplies (107).
2. The Office Supplies account is increasing (since they were purchased) and the Accounts Payable account is increasing (since the amount owed is going up).
3. The Office Supplies account is an asset, whose normal balance is a debit. The Accounts Payable account is a liability, whose normal balance is a credit.
4. The increasing Office Supplies account will be a debit and the increasing Accounts Payable account will be a credit.

The journal entry would be as follows:

General Journal				
Date	Description	PR	Debit	Credit
June 21	Office supplies	107	500	
	Account Payable, Barrie Business Supplies	201		500
	To record the purchase of office supplies on account			

Consider a business owner, John Doe, who wants to invest $50,000 into his business:

1. The accounts being affected are Cash (101) and Owner's Equity (301).
2. The Cash account is increasing (since the investment is money coming into the business) and the Owner's Equity account is increasing (since the investment gives the owner more equity in the business).
3. The Cash account is an asset, whose normal balance is a debit. The Owner's Equity account is an Equity account, whose normal balance is a credit.
4. The increasing Cash account will be a debit and the increasing Owner's Equity account will be a credit.

The journal entry for the transaction would be as follows:

General Journal				
Date	Description	PR	Debit	Credit
June 21	Cash	101	50,000	
	Capital, J. Doe	301		50,000
	To record an investment by John Doe			

Oppositely, John Doe wants to withdraw $50,000 from his business. "Owner's withdrawals" is a contra equity account:

1. The accounts being affected are Cash (101) and Owner's Withdrawals (302).
2. The Cash account is decreasing (since the withdrawal requires an outlay of cash) and the Owner's Withdrawals account is increasing (since the owner is withdrawing money).
3. The Cash account is an asset, whose normal balance is a debit. The Owner's Equity account is a contra equity account, whose normal balance is a debit.
4. The decreasing Cash account will be a credit and the increasing Owner's Equity account will be a debit.

The entry would be as follows:

General Journal				
Date	Description	PR	Debit	Credit
June 21	Withdrawals, J. Doe	302	50,000	
	Cash	101		50,000
	To record a withdrawal by John Doe			

Consider a **service organization** (a business that sells its time instead of inventory) that does work for a customer on June 21 and gets paid $500 in cash:

1. The accounts being affected are Cash (101) and Sales Revenue (401).
2. The Cash account is increasing (since the business received cash during the sale) and the Sales Revenue account is increasing (since the sale is a positive amount of revenue).
3. The Cash account is an asset, whose normal balance is a debit. The Sales Revenue account is a revenue account, whose normal balance is a credit.
4. The increasing Cash account will be a debit and the increasing Sales Revenue account will be a credit.

The journal entry would be as follows:

General Journal				
Date	Description	PR	Debit	Credit
June 21	Cash	101	500	
	Sales Revenue	401		500
	To record a revenue earned and received			

For this specific scenario, sales revenue was used. The type of revenue being used is specific to the transaction. For example, if rent is being collected, the revenue account would be rent revenue. If interest was being earned on an investment, the revenue account would be interest revenue.

Consider the same business but assume that it is a **merchandising organization**. A merchandising organization is a company that sells purchased or manufactured inventory. Assume that the business purchased $300 of inventory and then sold all of it for $500. Two entries need to be made. The first one is to record the sale (as shown in the previous example) and the second entry is to record the cost of the sale, which is the cost of the inventory. For this we use an account called **Cost of Goods Sold**. Recall the cost principle, which states that expenses are recorded in the same period as the revenue they generate. Therefore the cost of this inventory is not recorded until the inventory is sold. To record this entry:

1. The accounts being affected are Inventory (103) and Cost of Goods Sold (510).
2. The Inventory account is decreasing (since the business is selling inventory) and the Cost of Goods Sold account is increasing (since expense is now recognized).
3. The Inventory account is an asset, whose normal balance is a debit. The Cost of Goods Sold account is an expense, whose normal balance is a debit.
4. The increasing Cost of Goods Sold account will be a debit and the decreasing Inventory account will be a credit.

The journal entry would be as follows:

General Journal				
Date	Description	PR	Debit	Credit
June 21	Cost of Goods Sold	510	300	
	Inventory	103		300
	To record the cost of a sale			

Consider the same business from above, but assume that it is a service organization. That is, no inventory is involved. If the business got paid for the work on June 21, but did not perform the service until June 30, the entries would be a little different. Instead of having sales revenue, the account affected would be unearned revenue. It is unearned because even though the money has been received, the service has not yet been performed. The unearned revenue account is a liability since the business either owes the customer their money back or the service promised. The liability increases when the cash payment is received, and then decreases when either the revenue has been earned, or the cash is refunded. The June 21 transaction is to record the sale. Cash (asset) was received, so the account is increasing and is therefore debited. Unearned revenue (liability) is also increasing and is therefore credited. The June 30 transaction is to change the unearned revenue to sales revenue, signifying that the revenue has been earned. Unearned revenue (liability) is decreasing, so the account we will debited. Sales revenue (revenue) is increasing, so the account will be credited.

The reason that cash cannot be debited and revenue credited on June 21 (like in the situation where the revenue was earned at the time of payment) is because of the revenue recognition principle. As of June 21 revenue has not been *earned*, only that payment has been *received*. Until it is earned (something has been given in exchange for the payment or refunded the payment) it cannot be recorded it as revenue. The journal entries would be as follows:

General Journal				
Date	Description	PR	Debit	Credit
June 21	Cash	101	500	
	Unearned Revenue	206		500
	To record unearned revenue			
June 30	Unearned Revenue	206	500	
	Sales Revenue	401		500
	To record revenue earned and received			

If the reverse happens (where revenue is earned but payment has not been received), the revenue account can be credited since it has been earned. This would occur if the customer has paid on account and has agreed to come back and pay off their account at a later date. The increasing asset is not going to be cash since cash has not been received. Instead, the increasing asset (debit) is an account called **accounts receivable**. Like accounts payable, accounts receivable is used for short term purposes whereas notes receivable is used for long term. Assume that a customer receives services on June 21 in the amount of $500 and pays on account. Assume that the account was paid on June 30. Assume that the customer is Barrie Business Services. The first entry to record the sale would require a debit to the increasing accounts receivable (asset) and a credit to increasing sales revenue (revenue). The second entry to record the receipt of payment would require a debit to the increasing cash (asset) and a credit to the decreasing accounts receivable (asset). The journal entries would be as follows:

General Journal				
Date	Description	PR	Debit	Credit
June 21	Account Receivable, Barrie Business Services	102	500	
	Revenue	401		500
	To record revenue earned on account			
June 30	Cash	101	500	
	Account Receivable, Barrie Business Services	102		500
	To record a cash payment received			

Consider a company that has maintenance expenses of $250 which are paid on June 21 in cash. The entry would require a debit to the increasing maintenance expense (expense) and a credit the decreasing cash (asset). The entry would be as follows:

General Journal				
Date	Description	PR	Debit	Credit
June 21	Maintenance Expense	404	250	
	Cash	101		250
	To record the cash payment of maintenance expenses			

If the same maintenance expenses were paid on account on June 21 and the account was paid on June 30, then there would be two entries. The first one would be to record the payment of expenses on account. That entry would require a debit to the increasing maintenance expense (expense) and a credit to the increasing account payable (liability). For the second transaction, which is used to record the payment of the account, there will be a debit to the decreasing account payable (liability) and credit the decreasing cash (asset). Assume the company doing the maintenance work is called Barrie Business Services. The journal entries would be as follows:

General Journal				
Date	Description	PR	Debit	Credit
June 21	Maintenance Expenses	404	250	
	Account Payable, Barrie Business Services	201		250
	To record the payment of expenses on account			
June 30	Account Payable, Barrie Business Services	201	250	
	Cash	101		250
	To record a cash payment of an account payable			

When journalizing, the first step is to think about what accounts are being affected. Then, figure out if each of those accounts are increasing or decreasing. If the account is increasing, the normal balance is applied. If the account is decreasing, the opposite of the normal balance is applied. The reverse is true with contra accounts.

For income and expenses, the following chart shows commonly used **subaccounts** and the account to which they belong:

Account	Asset	Liability
Subaccount	Cash Accounts Receivable Prepaid Insurance Inventory Land / Building / Vehicle Any "Owned Investments"	Accounts payable Unearned revenue Mortgage Payable Notes Payable Payroll Taxes Payable Any "Owed Investments"

For assets and liabilities, the following chart shows commonly used subaccounts and the account to which they belong:

Account	Revenue	Expense
Subaccount	Sales Revenue Service Revenue Rental Revenue Interest Revenue	Utilities Expense Rent Expense Interest Expense Insurance Expense

For the equity account, the following chart shows what subaccounts are used, depending on the type of business:

Type of Business	Sole Proprietorship	Partnership	Corporation
Accounts	Owner's Investments Owner's Withdrawals	Partner's Investments Partner's Withdrawals	Common / Preferred Stock Dividends Paid

Posting Transactions

Once a journal entry has been posted to the general journal, it can then be posted to the general ledger. The difference between the journal and the ledger is that the journal is sorted chronologically by the transaction, whereas the ledger is sorted by account. On the ledger, each journal entry is picked apart and the accounts (along with their respective balance) are grouped together. Each individual line on the ledger is referenced to the journal entry from which it came, so that the journal entry can be easily found. This reference is a letter and a number code. The letter is "J" for journal and the number is the page number of the journal on which the transaction was posted. For example, if the transaction is on the first page of the journal, the code will be J1. This code will be placed in the PR column of the ledger next to the account that it is referencing. The following is an example of a general ledger.

General Ledger					Balance	
Date	Description	PR	Debit	Credit	Debit	Credit
(a)						
(b)	Opening Balance				(g)	(g)
(c)	(e)	(f)	(h)	(h)	(i)	(i)
(d)	Closing Balance				(j)	(j)

(a) The number and name of the account (i.e. 101 Cash)

(b) The date of the opening balance

(c) The date of the transaction.

(d) The date of the closing balance.

(e) The description for the specific transaction, also found on the general journal

(f) The post reference. This is the letter number code (i.e. J1)

(g) The debit *or* credit record of the opening balance

(h) The debit *or* credit record of the transaction

(i) The debit *or* credit record of new running total

(j) The debit *or* credit record of the closing balance

When the running total (also the balance of an account) is calculated, the previous running total is netted against the new transaction. For example, if the current balance in an account is a debit of $5,000, and a new transaction is a credit of $2,000, the new running total (balance) would be a debit of $3,000. The best way to illustrate posting entries is through an example. Below is the general journal showing some transactions of a company whose year end is December 31:

General Journal					
Date	Description	PR	Debit	Credit	
Jan. 6	Office Supplies		75		
	Cash			75	
	To record the cash purchase of office supplies				
Mar. 3	Cash		10,500		
	Capital, J. Doe			10,500	
	To record an investment by John Doe				
July 10	Cash		1,500		
	Rental Revenue			1,500	
	To record rental revenue received				
Sept. 6	Merchandise Inventory		500		
	Accounts Payable			500	
	To record inventory purchased on account				
Nov. 29	Telephone Expense		30		
	Cash			30	
	To record the cash payment of telephone expenses				

The first account is cash. On January 6 there was a $75 credit. On March 3 there was a $10,500 debit. On July 10 there was a debit of $1,500. On November 29 there was a credit of $30. Assuming that the opening balance on January 1 was $500, the general ledger for the cash account would be as follows:

General Ledger					Balance	
Date	Description	PR	Debit	Credit	Debit	Credit
101 Cash						
	Opening Balance		500		500	
Jan. 6	Purchase of supplies	J1		75	425	
Mar. 3	John Doe investment	J1	10,500		10,925	
July 10	Revenue received	J1	1,500		12,425	
Nov. 29	Telephone expenses paid	J1		30	12,395	
	Closing Balance				12,395	

Notice that the opening debit balance of $500 is netted against the $75 credit (from the January 6 transaction) to give a running total on January 6 of $425. This pattern continues through to the closing balance. In the following period, the opening balance for the cash account would be $12,395.

Below are the remaining accounts from the general journal from above. Assume that all of the remaining accounts have opening balances of $0.

General Ledger					Balance	
Date	Description	PR	Debit	Credit	Debit	Credit
102 Office Supplies						
	Opening Balance				0	
Jan. 6	Purchase of supplies	J1	75		75	
	Closing Balance				75	

General Ledger					Balance	
Date	Description	PR	Debit	Credit	Debit	Credit
103 Merchandise Inventory						
	Opening Balance				0	
Sept. 6	Account purchase of inventory	J1	500		500	
	Closing Balance				500	

General Ledger					Balance	
Date	Description	PR	Debit	Credit	Debit	Credit
201 Accounts Payable						
	Opening Balance					0
Sept. 6	Account purchase of inventory	J1		500		500
	Closing Balance					500

General Ledger					Balance	
Date	Description	PR	Debit	Credit	Debit	Credit
301 Capital, J. Doe						
	Opening Balance					0
Mar. 3	John Doe investment	J1		10,500		10,500
	Closing Balance					10,500

General Ledger						
Date	Description	PR	Debit	Credit	Balance	
					Debit	Credit
401 Rental Revenue						
	Opening Balance					0
Mar. 3	John Doe investment	J1		1,500		1,500
	Closing Balance					1,500

General Ledger						
Date	Description	PR	Debit	Credit	Balance	
					Debit	Credit
501 Telephone Expense						
	Opening Balance				0	
Nov. 29	Telephone expenses paid	J1	30		30	
	Closing Balance				30	

When looking at general ledger, the PR number will indicate the location of the journal entry where the transaction is recorded. When looking at the general journal, the PR number will indicate the account number so that it can be found in the general ledger. At this point the chart of accounts, general journal and general ledger are now complete. Therefore, the first three steps of the accounting cycle are also complete, and it is time to prepare a trial balance.

Chapter 3 – The Trial Balance

Unadjusted Trial Balance

Now that transactions have been posted to the general journal and the general ledger, it is time to prepare a trial balance. The trial balance is a list of each account and the corresponding balance. The process of creating a trial balance is to take each account as well as the final balance (on the last day of the reporting period) from the general ledger and list them on one statement known as the trial balance. The first step is to create an unadjusted trial balance. Consider the following accounts and balances which have been taken from a company's general ledger on the last day of the period:

Account	Closing Balance
101 – Cash	$505 (debit)
201 – Accounts Payable	$150 (credit)
301 – Capital, J. Doe	$200 (credit)
401 – Rental Revenue	$250 (credit)
501 – Telephone Expense	$95 (debit)

Based on the above accounts and balances, the unadjusted trial balance would appear as shown below. The totals should be added up at the bottom and they should balance. Thinking back to the journal entries, each transaction's debits and credits had to balance. Therefore the totals from those transactions (recorded in the general ledger and on the trial balance) should also balance.

Account No.	Account	Unadjusted Trial Balance		Adjustments		Adjusted Trial Balance	
		Debit	Credit	Debit	Credit	Debit	Credit
101	Cash	505					
201	Accounts Payable		150				
301	Capital, J. Doe		200				
401	Rental Revenue		250				
501	Telephone Expense	95					
	Totals	600	600				

(Company Name) Trial Balance As at (Current Date)

Adjusting Entries

Adjusting entries are used to accrue revenues and expenses. For example, consider a business that purchased three months of insurance (November 1 to January 31) on and paid for it upfront on November 1. This transaction will be recorded to the "pre-paid" insurance account. If their year end is December 31, it needs to be accounted for, that on December 31, two thirds of their insurance is no longer pre-paid. At that point, two thirds of the insurance must be expensed. This will require decreasing the prepaid insurance (asset) and increasing the insurance expense (expense). This adjusting entry would involve debiting insurance expense and crediting prepaid insurance in the amount of two thirds of the total.

There are two types of revenues and expenses that require adjusting entries. They are deferrals and accruals. Under deferrals, there are prepaid assets and expenses, unearned revenue and depreciation/amortization. Under accruals, there are accrued expenses and accrued revenues. Once the adjusting entries are complete, they will be posted to the general ledger and then added to the trial balance in the "adjusting entries" section. The date for every adjusting entry is the final date in whatever period that the entry is being recorded. Below are accounts and balances (debit or credit) of the journal entries, for the five types of adjusting entries. The bolded accounts in each entry are interchangeable (i.e. depreciation in the first example says "equipment" but it can be "automobile" or "machine" or any other capital asset)

1. Depreciation and Amortization

   Throughout a period, assets depreciate, and the amount by which they have depreciated must be accrued and recorded on the last day of the period. For example, if a piece of equipment depreciated by $2,000 this year, the books must show that depreciation. The journal (which is covered in the "Accounting for Assets" chapter) entry involves increasing the amortization expense (debit) increasing the accumulated amortization, which is a contra asset (credit). The entry would appear as follows:

General Journal				
Date	Description	PR	Debit	Credit
	Amortization Expense, **Equipment**		XXX	
	Accumulated Amortization, **Equipment**			XXX
	*To record the cash depreciation on **equipment***			

2. Prepaid Assets and Expenses

The adjusting entry for prepaid expenses is used to record use of an expense that was paid for in advance. For example, if year end is December 31 and six months of insurance is purchased on October 1, three months of the insurance will have been used and it will need to be taken out of the prepaid asset account and expensed. The adjusting entry for prepaid assets is used to record the use of assets previously purchased. The entry to record the use of a prepaid asset or expense involves increasing the expense (debit) and decreasing the asset (credit). The entries would appear as follows:

General Journal					
Date	Description	PR	Debit	Credit
Dec 31	**Insurance** Expense		XXX	
	Prepaid **Insurance**			XXX
	*To record the expired portion of the **insurance***			

3. Unearned Revenue

The adjusting entry for unearned revenue is used to record revenue that was previously unearned and now it is earned. For example, if a client pays for 6 months of work on October 1 and year end if December 31, then on December 31 3 months of that unearned revenue will have been earned. The entry to change unearned revenue into earned revenue involves decreasing the unearned revenue (debit) it and increasing revenue (credit). The entry would appear as follows:

General Journal					
Date	Description	PR	Debit	Credit
Dec 31	Unearned **Sales** Revenue		XXX	
	Sales Revenue			XXX
	To record the earned portion of unearned revenue			

4. Accrued Expenses

An accrued expense is a type of expense in a period that is unpaid and had not yet been recorded. For example, the interest on an interest bearing note payable is an accrued expense. It has not yet been paid, so it has not been recorded, but the liability has been incurred. To record the recognition of the liability, an entry needs to be created that will expense the accrued interest to date but also recognize that it has not been paid (using a payable account). The adjusting entry to record the recognition of an accrued expense becoming a liability, involves increasing the expense (debit) and increasing the payable (credit). The entry would appear as follows:

General Journal					
Date	Description	PR	Debit	Credit
	Interest Expense		XXX	
	Interest Payable			XXX
	To record an accrued interest expense			

5. Accrued Revenues

Like accrued expenses, accrued revenues are revenues that have neither been recorded nor received. For example, consider the interest bearing note example from above, except as the recipient of the interest. Any interest that has accrued during the period must be recorded as an asset. The entry to record accrued revenue involves increasing the receivable (debit) and increasing the revenue (credit). The entry would appear as follows:

General Journal					
Date	Description	PR	Debit	Credit
	Interest Receivable		XXX	
	Interest Revenue			XXX
	To record an accrued revenue			

Using the above information, consider a company that pays $2,000 cash on March 20 for 3 months of insurance. The coverage is for April 1 to May 31. The company has monthly periods ending on the last day of each month. Given the above information, the journal entries (the entry to record the purchase of the insurance and the two adjusting entries to record the expiration of insurance) would appear as follows:

General Journal					
Date	Description	PR	Debit	Credit
Mar 20	Prepaid Insurance		2,000	
	Cash			2,000
	To record the purchase of prepaid insurance			
Apr 30	Insurance Expense		1,000	
	Prepaid Insurance			1,000
	To record an adjusting entry for use of prepaid insurance			
May 31	Insurance Expense		1,000	
	Prepaid Insurance			1,000
	To record an adjusting entry for use of prepaid insurance			

Back to the trial balance, the sums of the adjusting entries will be placed in the middle columns. Assume that the trial balance is for April 30 where only 1 month of insurance has been used. Also assume that the company has an opening balance in the cash account of $3,000 and a note payable of $5,000. From the journal entries above, the first entry will not be in the adjustments column. It is only a transaction to record the purchase of the insurance and that would have occurred during the period. In this case it occurred on March 20. The opening cash balance would already have incorporated the $2000 insurance purchase. Since the second adjusting entry has not occurred yet, so it will not be on this trial balance. The opening balance for prepaid insurance is a debit of $2,000. Below is what the trial balance so far would look like:

(Company Name) Trial Balance As at April 30, XXXX							
Account No.	Account	Unadjusted Trial Balance		Adjustments		Adjusted Trial Balance	
		Debit	Credit	Debit	Credit	Debit	Credit
	Cash	3,000					
	Prepaid Insurance	2,000			1,000		
	Note Payable		5,000				
	Insurance Expense			1,000			
		5,000	5,000	1,000	1,000		

Adjusted Trial Balance

The last step of the trial balance is to prepare the adjusted trial balance. To do this, simply take the values of the unadjusted column and net them against the adjustments column. As an example, consider the following trial balance:

Account No.	Account	Unadjusted Trial Balance		Adjustments		Adjusted Trial Balance	
		Debit	Credit	Debit	Credit	Debit	Credit
	Cash	5,000		2,500			
	Notes Payable		2,500	1,000			
	Capital, J. Doe		2,500		3,500		
	Sales Revenue		1,000				
	Rent Expense	1,000					
		6,000	6,000	3,500	3,500		

(Company Name)
Trial Balance
As at December 31, XXXX

For example, the balance on the unadjusted trial balance is a debit of $5,000 and the adjusting entry is a debit of $2,500. Therefore the adjusted amount is a debit of $7,500. The trial balance given the changes would be as follows:

Account No.	Account	Unadjusted Trial Balance		Adjustments		Adjusted Trial Balance	
		Debit	Credit	Debit	Credit	Debit	Credit
	Cash	5,000		2,500		7,500	
	Notes Payable		2,500	1,000			1,500
	Capital, J. Doe		2,500		3,500		6,000
	Sales Revenue		1,000				1,000
	Rent Expense	1,000				1,000	
		6,000	6,000	3,500	3,500	8,500	8,500

(Company Name)
Trial Balance
As at December 31, XXXX

Using the final amounts from the adjusted trial balance, the financial statements can be created. All of the asset, liability and equity accounts will go on the balance sheet while the revenue and expense accounts will go on the income statement.

Chapter 4 – Financial Statements
Income Statement

Creating financial statements is largely the most important part of accounting. All of the information that has been entered and prepared thus far culminates to preparing the financial statements. Financial statements are used by the accounting department (for financial forecasting) and by the owner (to see how their business is doing) and by the creditors (to measure the risk of lending money to the business) and by current and prospective investors (to evaluate the risks and returns of investing in the business). The financial statements have to be prepared in a specific order starting with the income statement. The net income calculated on the income statement is then used to prepare the statement of changes in equity. The owner's equity at the end of the period will be included on the balance sheet. Therefore, the income statement is prepared first, followed by statement of changes in equity, and then the balance sheet.

For the purposes of this book, the single-step income statement will be prepared as it is most commonly used for small businesses. The income statement is used to measure the net income or net loss of a business. Net income occurs when the revenues exceed the expenses and net loss occurs when the expenses exceed the revenues. Every financial statement has a three line heading at the top of the page similar to the trial balance. The first line is always the name of the company. The second line is the name of the financial statement. The third line is the date of the statement. The format of the third line will vary based on the statement. If the statement is measuring its contents at a specific date, it will show "As at (date)" but if it is measuring the contents over a period of time, it will show "For the period (i.e. year/quarter/month/etc.) ended (date)". Recall that the trial balance was recording the balances of each account on the last day of the period. Therefore, it showed "As at (last day of the period)". The income statement is recording all revenues and expenses over a period. Therefore it will show "For the (period) ended (last day of period)". The income statement has two headings: "Revenues" and "Expenses". At the bottom, the sum of the expenses is subtracted from the sum of the revenues to present the net income or net loss. In accounting, when a number is in parenthesis, it means that the number is negative.

Consider Company ABC, a sole proprietorship, whose year end is December 31. The company has investments where they earn interest and they sublet a portion of their office space. Their only expenses are utilities on the office space and salaries/wages for their employees. The following is the company's adjusted trial balance (for the 20X3 year) showing only the revenue and expense accounts:

Account No.	Account	Unadjusted Trial Balance		Adjustments		Adjusted Trial Balance	
		Debit	Credit	Debit	Credit	Debit	Credit
	Sales Revenue						100,000
	Rental Revenue						25,000
	Interest Revenue						5,000
	Utilities Expense					25,000	
	Salaries / Wages					65,000	

Company ABC — Trial Balance — As at December 31, XXXX

The following is an income statement prepared for the 20X3 year:

Company ABC
Income Statement
For the year ended 31 Dec. 20X3

Revenues		
Sales Revenue	$100,000	
Rental Revenue	$25,000	
Interest Revenue	$5,000	
Total Revenue		$130,000
Expenses		
Utilities Expense	$25,000	
Salaries and Wages Expense	$65,000	
Total Expenses		$90,000
Net Income/(Loss)		$40,000

Note the two columns. The left column is used to list all of the accounts and the right column is used for the totals. The last account before the subtotal underlined, and the total at the bottom is double underlined. If the business incurred a net loss, the bottom number would be in parenthesis. This is what the income statement for most small businesses would look like. When preparing the statement of changes in equity, the net income from this statement will be used.

Statement of Changes in Equity

A statement of changes in equity, like the income statement, is measured over a period of time. Instead of measuring how much the business earned and spent, it will measure how much the owner's/partners' equity in the business has changed. The first line is the equity at the beginning of the period. This number is the ending equity from the previous period. If it is the businesses' first period in operations, the number is $0. To that amount any investments by the owner/partners is added. The net income (if any) is added, or the net loss (if any) is subtracted. To that amount any withdrawals by the owner/partners is subtracted. Finally, all of the above is totalled showing the ending equity.

Consider Company ABC (a sole proprietorship) from above. Recall their net income was $40,000 and their year-end was December 31. The equity at the beginning of the year was $50,000. The owner, Ralph Smith, invested $30,000 into the business throughout 2013 and also withdrew $12,000 in the same year. The following is a statement of changes in equity for 20X3.

Company ABC Statement of Changes in Equity For the year ended 31 Dec. 20X3		
R. Smith, capital, 1 Jan. 20X3		$50,000
Add: Owner's Investments	$30,000	
Add: Net Income	$40,000	$70,000
Total		$120,000
Less: Owner's Withdrawals		$12,000
R. Smith, capital, 31 Dec. 20X3		$108,000

Consider the same business and same circumstances, except instead of a net income of $40,000, assume that the business had a net loss of $40,000. The statement would be as follows:

Company ABC Statement of Changes in Equity For the year ended 31 Dec. 20X3		
R. Smith, capital, 1 Jan. 20X3		$50,000
Add: Owner's Investments		$30,000
Total		$80,000
Less: Owner's Withdrawals	$12,000	
Less: Net Loss	$40,000	$52,000
R. Smith, capital, 31 Dec. 20X3		$28,000

Balance Sheet

The balance sheet measures what assets the business owns as well as what the business owes to its owners and debtors at a given point in time. Since it is at one point in time, the heading will read "As at (last day of period)". The balance sheet lists assets on the left and liabilities and equity on the right. To represent this relationship, there is what is called **the accounting equation**, which is "Assets = Liabilities + Equity." At the bottom of the balance sheet, the total assets should therefore equal the sum of the total liabilities and equity.

Consider Company ABC from above (with the net income, not the net loss). Recall the owner's equity at year-end was 108,000 and their year-end was December 31. The following is the company's adjusted trial balance (for the 20X3 year) showing only the asset and liability accounts:

<table>
<tr><td colspan="8" align="center">Company ABC
Trial Balance
As at December 31, XXXX</td></tr>
<tr><td rowspan="2">Account No.</td><td rowspan="2">Account</td><td colspan="2">Unadjusted Trial Balance</td><td colspan="2">Adjustments</td><td colspan="2">Adjusted Trial Balance</td></tr>
<tr><td>Debit</td><td>Credit</td><td>Debit</td><td>Credit</td><td>Debit</td><td>Credit</td></tr>
<tr><td></td><td>Cash</td><td></td><td></td><td></td><td></td><td>70,000</td><td></td></tr>
<tr><td></td><td>Accounts Receivable</td><td></td><td></td><td></td><td></td><td>35,000</td><td></td></tr>
<tr><td></td><td>Equipment</td><td></td><td></td><td></td><td></td><td>40,000</td><td></td></tr>
<tr><td></td><td>Accounts Payable</td><td></td><td></td><td></td><td></td><td></td><td>5,000</td></tr>
<tr><td></td><td>Mortgage Payable</td><td></td><td></td><td></td><td></td><td></td><td>32,000</td></tr>
</table>

Given the above information, the balance sheet would be as follows:

<table>
<tr><td colspan="4" align="center">Company ABC
Balance Sheet
As at 31 Dec. 20X3</td></tr>
<tr><td>Assets</td><td></td><td>Liabilities</td><td></td></tr>
<tr><td>Cash</td><td>$70,000</td><td>Accounts Payable</td><td>$5,000</td></tr>
<tr><td>Accounts Receivable</td><td>$35,000</td><td>Mortgage Payable</td><td>$32,000</td></tr>
<tr><td>Equipment</td><td>$40,000</td><td>Total Liabilities</td><td>$37,000</td></tr>
<tr><td></td><td>145,000</td><td></td><td></td></tr>
<tr><td></td><td></td><td>Equity</td><td></td></tr>
<tr><td></td><td></td><td>R. Smith, capital</td><td>$108,000</td></tr>
<tr><td>Total Assets</td><td>$145,000</td><td>Total Liabilities and Equity</td><td>$145,000</td></tr>
</table>

No matter which column is longer, the totals must be on the same line. Each side has two columns with the left side used for individual accounts and the right side for totals. The above is a very simplified version of the balance sheet whereas it is not uncommon for a small business to group assets and liabilities based on the type of account. If assets and liabilities are grouped based on the type of account, it is called a **classified balance sheet**. The balance sheet from above has been converted to a classified balance sheet, as shown below:

Company ABC Balance Sheet As at 31 Dec. 20X3					
Assets			Liabilities		
Current Assets			Current Liabilities		
Cash	$70,000		Accounts Payable	$5,000	
Accounts Receivable	$35,000		Total Current Liabilities		$5,000
Total Current Assets		$105,000			
			Long Term Liabilities		
PPE			Mortgage Payable	$32,000	
Equipment	$40,000		Total Long Term Liabilities		$32,000
Total PPE		$40,000	Total Liabilities		$37,000
			Equity		
			R. Smith, capital		$108,000
Total Assets		$145,000	Total Liabilities and Equity		$145,000

Note: Refer to the first section of chapter one for the types of assets and liabilities.

Cash Flows and Cash Flow Statement

The **cash flow statement** is a statement that is used to determine, how much cash is actually coming in to the business, and how much is leaving. It is different from the income statement in that it tracks official cash receipts and outlays rather than revenues and expenses. For example, the income statement would show an amortization expense. An amortization expense does not involve an outlay of cash and the cash flow statement would account for that. To prepare a cash flow statement, it is necessary to have the balance sheet from the current and previous reporting periods, which can be amalgamated into a statement called the comparative balance sheet. It is also necessary to complete the income statement for the current period, as the net income is the first line of the cash flow statement. After that point, four rules will be applied:

1. <u>Subtract an increase in non-cash current assets</u>. As assets are purchased, an outlay of cash is required. The only exception is if the assets were received for free (i.e. won, inheritance, donation, etc.).

2. <u>Add a decrease in non-cash current assets</u>. As assets are sold, an inflow of cash is experienced. The only exception is if the assets were disposed of with no residual value (i.e. thrown away, stolen or destroyed with no insurance, donated, etc.).

3. <u>Add an increase in liabilities</u>. When a liability is incurred, there is also an expense to go along with it (for example, purchasing office supplies on account).

4. <u>Subtract a decrease in liabilities</u>. When a liability is satisfied (that is, a debt is paid) there is an outlay of cash and as such cash is decreasing.

To prepare a comparative balance sheet, the first step is to take the net amounts of each asset and list them on the new balance sheet. The cost less any contra account (i.e. asset cost, less accumulated depreciation) is the net amount. The amount section of the balance sheet should have be two columns, where the first column is the current amount and the second column is the previous amount.

Below is an example of a 20X3 and 20X4 comparative balance sheet for a company that prepares their financial statements yearly:

Company ABC Comparative Balance Sheet As at 31 Dec. 20X3 and 31 Dec. 20X4		
	20X4	20X3
Assets		
Current Assets		
Cash	$15,000	$5,000
Accounts Receivable	$6,000	$5,000
Total Current Assets	$21,000	$10,000
Property, Plant and Equipment		
Company Vehicle	$15,000	$30,000
Total Property, Plant and Equipment	$15,000	$30,000
Total Assets	$36,000	$40,000
Liabilities		
Current Liabilities		
Unearned Revenue	$3,800	$4,100
Accounts Payable	$3,200	$3,200
Total Current Liabilities	$7,000	$7,300
Long Term Liabilities		
Mortgage Payable		$10,000
Bonds Payable	$12,500	$9,000
Total Long Term Liabilities	$12,500	$19,000
Total Liabilities	$19,500	$26,300
Equity		
Owner's Equity	$16,500	$13,700
Total Equity	$16,500	$13,700
Total Liabilities and Equity	$36,000	$40,000

Based on the above comparative balance sheet, a cash flow statement can be produced. Assume the company had a no gains or losses, an amortization expense of $7,500 and a net income of $11,700 for 20X4. Also assume the owner did not invest or withdraw any money from the business throughout the year.

The following is the corresponding cash flow statement:

Company ABC Statement of Cash Flows For the Year Ended 31 Dec. 20X4		
Operating Activities: Net Income (Earnings After Taxes)		$11,700
Add items not requiring an outlay of cash: Amortization		$7,500
Cash flow from operations		$19,200
Changes in non-cash working capital: Decrease in unearned revenue Increase in accounts receivable	$300 ($1,000)	
Net change in non-cash working capital		($700)
Cash provided by (used in) operating activities		$18,500
Investing Activities: Decrease in plant and equipment	$15,000	
Cash used in investing activities		$15,000
Financing Activities: Increase in bonds payable Decrease in mortgage payable	$3,500 ($10,000)	
Cash used in financing activities		($6,500)
Net increase (decrease) in cash during the year:		$10,000
Cash, beginning of the year		$5,000
Cash, end of year		$15,000

Notice that unlike the income statement, where the last line is the net income/loss, the net income is the starting point. From this point on, the purpose of every adjustment will be to convert net income/loss to net inflow/outlay of cash. First, the amortization expense is added. Amortization expense was subtracted on the income statement and since it does not involve an outlay of cash, it can be added back.

The next three sections will be cash provided by/used in operating activities, investing activities and financing activities. Operating activities will include all non-cash current assets and current liabilities. Investing activities will include all non-current assets and financing activities will include all non-current liabilities. Notice that because the accounts payable account did not change, it was not included on the cash flow statement. The dollar value of change of cash would be $0 so it would not affect the statement balance in any way. In 20X4 the mortgage was fully paid off, so the amount ($0) was left off the balance sheet for that year.

Furthermore, notice that the cash balance in 20X3 was $5,000 and the cash balance in 20X4 was $15,000. There was a net change of $10,000 in the cash account during the 20X4 year. The cash flow statement reconciles this change as shown in the last three lines.

If the owner withdrew money from the business, it would be included in financing activities. It would read "increase in owner's withdrawals" and the amount that the owner withdrew would be subtracted from the total. It would be subtracted, because the owner taking money out of the business involves the business experiencing an outlay of cash.

If the owner invested money into the business, it would also appear in financing activities. It would read "increase in owner's investment" and the amount that the owner invested would be added to the total. It would be added, because the business owner investing money into the business involves with business experiencing an inflow of cash.

If the business had a gain or loss on an asset, that would also be shown on the cash flow statement. For example, consider a company that purchases a vehicle for $30,000 to do deliveries. If the vehicle depreciated such that it had a residual value of $6,000, but it was sold for $7,500, there would be a "gain on sale of vehicle" in the amount of $1,500. On the cash flow statement, a sale of $7,500 under investing activity would be added. It is added because the sale of the vehicle resulted in an inflow of cash. The $1,500 gain would be subtracted in the operating activities section. It is subtracted because it has been included twice: Once in the net income, and again in the sale of vehicle in investing activity.

Chapter 5 – Closing Accounts

Closing Entries

After preparing financial statements, there is one last step to the accounting cycle. The temporary accounts have to be closed. That is, the balance of the accounts needs to be set to zero. Accounts found on the balance sheet are permanent accounts, whereas accounts found on the income statement are temporary accounts. The purpose of closing accounts at the end of a period is so that when transactions are recorded for the next period, they will not have entries and balances from the previous period. The revenue and expense accounts are closed to the income summary account and then the income summary and withdrawals accounts are closed to the owner's capital account. Closing entries are done on the last day of the period.

Consider the following financial statements for the first year of operations (20X2) for Company XYZ, a sole proprietorship owned by Christian Moore with a December 31, year-end:

Company XYZ Income Statement For the year ended 31 Dec. 20X2		
Revenues		
Sales Revenue	$65,000	
Interest Revenue	$5,000	
Total Revenue		$70,000
Expenses		
Supplies Expense	$7,500	
Wages Expense	$2,500	
Utilities Expense	$30,000	
Total Expenses		$40,000
Net Income/(Loss)		$30,000

Company XYZ Statement of Changes in Equity For the year ended 31 Dec. 20X2		
C. Moore, capital, 1 Jan. 20X2		$25,000
Add: Owner's Investments	$35,000	
Add: Net Income	$30,000	$65,000
Total		$90,000
Less: Owner's Withdrawals		$20,000
R. Smith, capital, 31 Dec. 20X2		$70,000

The first accounts to close are the revenue accounts, which need to be closed to the income summary account. Since the normal balance of a revenue account is a credit, it will need to be debited by the balance in the account. This will set the account balance to zero. The closing journal entry would appear as follows:

General Journal					
Date	Description	PR	Debit	Credit
Dec. 31	Sales Revenue		65,000	
	Interest Revenue		5,000	
	Income Summary			70,000
	To close the revenue accounts to income summary			

The next accounts to close are the expense accounts, which need to be closed to the income summary account. Since the normal balance of an expense account is a debit, it will need to be credited by the balance in the account. This will set the account balance to zero. The closing journal entry would appear as follows:

General Journal					
Date	Description	PR	Debit	Credit
Dec. 31	Income Summary		40,000	
	Supplies Expense			7,500
	Wages Expense			2,500
	Utilities Expense			30,000
	To close the expense accounts to income summary			

When the revenue accounts were closed to income summary, the income summary account had a credit balance of $70,000. When the expense accounts were closed to income summary, the income summary account had a debit of $40,000. When the two balances were netted against each other, the income summary account is left with a credit balance of $30,000. Notice that this balance is equal to the company's net income. The next step is to close the income summary account to the owner's capital account. Since the income summary account has a credit balance of $30,000, it will need to be debited by that amount and then the owner's capital will be credited by the same amount. The closing journal entry would appear as follows:

General Journal					
Date	Description	PR	Debit	Credit
Dec. 31	Income Summary		30,000	
	Owner's Capital			30,000
	To close income summary to owner's capital			

Finally, the owner's withdrawals account needs to be closed to owner's capital. Currently, the balance in the withdrawals account is a debit of $20,000. Therefore it will be credited by that amount to set the balance to zero, and owner's capital will be debited by $20,000. The closing journal entry would appear as follows:

General Journal					
Date	Description	PR	Debit	Credit
Dec. 31	Owner's Capital		20,000	
	Withdrawals			20,000
	To close withdrawals to owner's capital			

Notice the progression of closing accounts. The revenue accounts and expense accounts netted against each other show the business' (positive or negative) income. The business' income and the owner's withdrawals netted against each other shows how much equity is left in the business.

Post-Close Trial Balance

The last step in closing accounts is to prepare a post-close trial balance. The post-close trial balance is easier than the adjusted trial balance in that there are fewer accounts to be included. Only the permanent accounts go on the post-close trial balance, since the temporary accounts have a zero balance now that they have been closed.

Consider Company XYZ from above with an equity balance on December 31, 20X2 of $70,000. Their post-close trial balance is shown below, given that they had the following accounts:

Cash: $35,000

Accounts Receivable: $60,000

Equipment: $10,000

Mortgage Payable: $30,000

Unearned Revenue: $5,000

Company XYZ Post-Close Trial Balance As at 31 Dec. 20X2			
Account No.	Account	Debit	Credit
	Cash	$35,000	
	Accounts Receivable	$60,000	
	Equipment	$10,000	
	Mortgage Payable		$30,000
	Unearned Revenue		$5,000
	R. Smith, capital, 31 Dec. 20X2		$70,000
	Totals	105,000	105,000

Now that the post-close trial balance is done, the accounting cycle is now complete!

Glossary

Term	Definition
Account	Asset, Liability, Equity, Revenue and Expense
Accounting Cycle	The full cycle during which all of a business' transactions are turned into meaningful documents
Accounts Receivable	An account for short term loans
Accrual Basis Accounting	The process of recording revenues when they are earned and recording expenses when they are owed
Adjusting Entry	Entries used to make adjustments to accounts on the trial balance
Amortization	The amount by which an intangible asset loses value
Asset	An item, tangible or intangible, that has economic value
Balance Sheet	A statement reflecting what the business owns and what the business owes
Business Entity Principle	The transactions that a business records, must not represent the personal transactions of the owner(s). For example, an owner cannot list the amount they spend on clothes as an expense on the business' income statement.
Capital Asset	See Property, Plant and Equipment
Cash Basis Accounting	The process of recording revenues when they are received and recording expenses when they are paid
Cash Flow Statement	A statement showing the actual cash flow of a business, rather than revenues and expenses
Chart of Accounts	A list of all the accounts and the corresponding account numbers
Closing Entry	Entries used to close temporary accounts at the end of a period
Consistency Principle	The same accounting methods must be used period after period. A company that uses one method to calculate the cost of inventory in January must use the same method in February. This allows readers to make comparisons throughout several different periods.
Contra Account	The opposite of the typical of expected balance of an account
Corporation	A business that has one or more owners is a separate legal entity
Cost Principle	Financial statement information to be based on the cost of a specific transaction. For example, if a car is purchased for $10, 000 but has a market value of $15, 000, the cost principle requires that $10, 000 be recorded.
Current Asset	An asset that is either cash or easily liquidated
Current Liability	A short term liability. Typically less than one year
Depreciation	The amount by which a tangible asset loses value
Double Entry Accounting	An accounting system that uses debits and credits, which must balance by having at least two entries in each transaction
Equity	The amount of a business' assets to which the owner(s) is/are entitled
Expenses	Money that is spent for a business to operate and earn revenue
Fiscal Year	The time period during which a full accounting cycle occurs
Full Disclosure Principle	Financial statements must include all relevant information. If a business experienced a loss in one of its departments, the full disclosure principle prevents the owner from leaving that loss off the books

Term	Definition
General Journal	A journal in which all of a business' transactions are posted
General Ledger	The statement on which all journal entries are posted
Generally Accepted Accounting Principles (GAAP)	A series of accounting principles used to govern accountants
Gross Income	The sum of all an employee's earnings in a given period
Income Statement	A statement reflecting the business' revenues, expenses and net income
Intangible Asset	An asset that it not tangible such as a patent
Inventory	Merchandise owned by the company that has not been sold yet
Investments	A financial stake made in an entity, often in exchange for equity
Journal Entry	An entry made in the general journal to record a transactions
Liability	A future obligation resulting from a current transaction
Long-Term Asset	See Property, Plant and Equipment
Long Term Liability	A liability that is typically longer than one year, such as a mortgage
Matching Principle	Expenses must be reported in the same period as the revenues that were earned
Materiality Principle	Amounts may be left out of the financial statements if they will not be of interest to the reader. For example, if a business spent $1 on a stamp.
Merchandise Organization	An organization that primarily sells merchandise
Net Income / Loss	The total revenues less the total expenses
Normal Balance	The typical or expected balance of an account
Owner's Equity	The equity account used for a sole proprietorship
Partners' Equity	The equity account used for a partnership
Partnership	A business that has more than one owner and unlimited legal liability
Petty Cash	A small fund kept on hand for small purchases to eliminate having to enter immaterial transactions
Property, Plant and Equipment	An asset that is not easy to liquidate. It often has a deed and it depreciates/amortizes.
Revenue	Money that is generated from a business' activities
Revenue Recognition Principle	Revenue must be recorded at the time it is earned (when the good is delivered or the service is rendered), not when the payment is received.
Service Organization	An organization that primarily sells its time
Shareholders' Equity	The equity account used for a corporation
Sole Proprietorship	A business that has one owner and unlimited legal liability
Source Documents	Documents that are kept as a record of a transactions
Stakeholders	People who are affected by the actions of a business
Statement of Changes in Equity	A statement reflecting the amount of equity the/each owner has
Subaccount	A more specific account within one of the five main accounts.
Trial Balance	A list of all accounts and their balances as well as adjustments
Timeliness Principle	The business' transactions must be reported on a consistent basis. For example, quarterly, monthly or annually.

www.ingramcontent.com/pod-product-compliance
Lightning Source LLC
Chambersburg PA
CBHW080619180526
45168CB00007B/2981